Advanced
Magic

GENEVIEVE DAVIS

Disclaimer: The author bears no responsibility for any consequences resulting from the use of information provided in this book. Please use all information at your own risk. No part of this publication may be reproduced or transmitted in any form without the express permission of the author.

Advanced Magic

A Course in Manifesting an Exceptional Life

Book 3

Genevieve Davis

Author's Note

In keeping with my current commitment not to make direct financial gain from teaching Magic, I will be donating the profits from this book to the Cotton Tree Children's Trust Orphanage, Freetown, Sierra Leone.

CONTENTS

1 WHAT NEXT?

So you have read *Becoming Magic* and *Doing Magic*. As you are now reading the third book in the series, I take it that you got something worthwhile from those first volumes. Maybe you found them a fun read, a nice way to spend an afternoon, a pleasant way to kill an hour or two. But it's just possible you found them more valuable than mere entertainment. As you were reading, did it feel like something inside you sat up and listened? Did it seem that the author knew your mind? Did the books talk about thoughts and feelings you have had but never articulated?

Did the words describe your experience so acutely that they seemed to have been written especially for you personally? Did it feel that the author was talking to you and only you? Did you sometimes think *I could have written this myself?*

Something deep inside you awoke. Something that had lain dormant, sleeping, lost under years of unhappiness and negativity. A glowing excitement. A sense of wonder and anticipation. A childlike awe at the possibility that was now before you.

Did you feel that?

A sparkling aliveness

A sense of the extraordinary

A glimpse of Magic

That was real

It's starting. You are waking up. You are opening your eyes and seeing the sun again. You are *Becoming Magic.*

Feeling inspired, you diligently followed the instructions to clear your thoughts of negativity: not complaining, staying positive, and seeing the good in all things. And you almost certainly *had some success.*

Just by following those first two books, you doubtless saw some really amazing changes in the direction of an exceptional life.

But at some point, perhaps it all started to feel a little less exciting – the buzz started to wear off. Was it all an illusion? You *think* you made some wonderful things happen, but you can't seem to replicate them. If only your manifestations could be a little more... reliable. You want nothing more than to rekindle that feeling you had when you read my first two books. *Why can't you feel like that all the time?*

I want you to know that whatever you felt, *that was real.* And with practise, you can feel like that almost every moment of your life.

Stay with this. Stay with me. Continue the journey

It's time to think a little deeper, feel a little keener, experience a little more intensely, and so consolidate and strengthen your knowledge. Everything in those first books still holds, but that was only the beginning. You've had your dabble. You've had your paddle. Now it's time for the real stuff.

In many ways, there is nothing new in this book. The principles haven't changed, and everything I have said in the course so far still holds. What I present to you is a deepening, a cementing of those first short lessons.

This book is designed to increase the fledgling power that you discovered from the first two books of the course. We now need to *build* on what has gone before, strengthening your resolve and rekindling your sense of Magic.

This book is the next step on the path to becoming a true creator of your own exceptional life.

2 WHY DO I KNOW SO MUCH ABOUT IT?

I was born with an amazing special ability – the ability to do Magic. I had an underlying sense of goodness, positivity and an innate power to affect everything around me – I could get anything I wanted. I was born a creator, a powerful wizard, a god.

And here's the brilliant thing...

...*so were you!*

It is my belief that we are all born with the ability to do Magic. Once upon a time, you were probably quite proficient in getting anything you wanted.

Many of us can remember that time. In this course, I'm not giving you anything you don't already have. I'm not even teaching you anything you don't already know. I'm simply encouraging you to notice and acknowledge the great powers that *already lie within you.*

Once upon a time, *you knew all this.*

So rather than asking how we do Magic, perhaps a better question would be *how do we get it so wrong?*

I have always loved to spend my Sunday mornings reading. I remember many a happy weekend when I would download a suitable book to my Kindle on a Sunday morning, sit in a coffee shop and spend a leisurely couple of hours reading it. I'd get all buzzed up from the motivational power of the writing (and from the caffeine!) I would feel on top of the world, and for those few hours in the coffee shop, I really believed that my life was about to change.

Usually, after a week (or less) of 'positive thinking', journal-keeping, non-complaining and other worthwhile changes, the buzz had worn off, and all those positive steps had begun to look a bit too much like hard work. I would start letting things go and begin slipping back into my old ways. Something 'bad' or unexpected would come along, and I would become despondent, declare 'it doesn't work' and move on to a new book, course, or system.

But one Sunday was different. The oft-repeated motto had been ringing around in my head: *if you keep doing what you're doing, you'll keep getting what you're getting.* This has to be one of the simplest but most profoundly meaningful sound bites I have ever come across.

And that moment I realised: if I didn't do something *radically* different, nothing would ever change in my mediocre life. Something *clicked*, and I have never seen the world in quite the same way again.

I realised I was just reading for fun, having a quick attempt at the instructions given, then letting everything go once I got bored or distracted. I was acting as if I could change my life just through the act of reading – as if the books I read contained enchanted words or spells. I wasn't properly studying, committing, or working at this. I expected massive change but wasn't putting in massive effort. It would be more accurate to describe my actions as 'messing around'. So this time, it really *had* to be different. The games were over and the work had begun.

I committed, *fully,* to changing my life. I made a declaration, much like the one I ask you to make in *Becoming Magic,* and stuck it on my wall and on the desktop of my computer. I *knew* I was still feeling that *buzz* that always accompanies making a new start. But this time, when that buzz wore off, as it inevitably does, I pushed on through and past – *I kept going,* and in doing so I took my Magical ability to another level.

When I started to become even remotely proficient at using Magic, I soon got to the stage where I felt I wanted to push things. I didn't need to manifest any more stuff, but I did fancy the idea of becoming more masterful, more controlled in my Magic, more *powerful.* Perhaps like you, my manifestations were often still unpredictable, almost random. Sometimes, the easiest tiny thing seemed impossible to attain, while the really huge things seemed to come to me easily. My life was full and prosperous, but I still felt like a child in control of a powerful weapon.

Sometimes I still felt unworthy, like I was playing with things to which I had no right, a fraud. I wanted to feel, not like a naughty girl who had stolen her master's wand, but like a true sorcerer myself.

So I threw myself fully and wholeheartedly into studying Magic, but I read no more books. The object of my study was *me* – my life and my experience. I went from following instructions blindly to paying attention to what goes on *in me* and *for me* when I am doing these things. I have gone from 'trying things out' to making these things my life.

The source of Magic is YOU, not the book, not the course, not the words, not the other person.

I have noticed the way things change when I have changed. I have noticed that when I push, grasp, and long for something, I almost never get it. I have noticed that when I spend my day wondering and obsessing over an apparent problem, it remains unresolved.

I have noticed the way that properly accessing the *receiving state* will often bring about the rapid manifestation of my desire or the resolution of a problem. I have learned that when I stop trying to force things to happen, they generally come to me.

I have looked out for subtle changes in me, in my life, in my experience. I have watched, watched, watched myself, never once questioning why things weren't working or becoming despondent that some mishap had befallen me.

In doing this, I have discovered that it is possible to see a good side in almost any apparent disaster. (If you did no more than try to see the good in all things, your life would change in fantastical ways.)

These days, I walk around in a state of what I describe as 'delicious expectation'. By living from a place of profound non-pushing, non-forcing, and non-grasping, I no longer see life and the world as something that happens *to* me. There is no pushing, no resisting, no worry or disappointment. I dance with it.

Life doesn't just happen to me. *We happen together.*

3 WHAT IS ADVANCED MAGIC?

One of the great fallacies often told often about Magic and the Law of Attraction is that using it is *easy*, simple, as easy as 1-2-3.

'Anyone can do it. It is the easiest thing in the whole Universe. After all, you are using it every moment of the day anyway, so it's just a matter of a subtle change in focus and every thing you want will fall into your lap.'

It should be perfectly obvious to anyone who has experimented with Magic that this is nonsense.

Attracting things into your life is not the same as Magic. We all attract things. We have all made things happen from time to time. But being really, truly in control of making things happen, attracting things *at will,* using Magic consistently and reliably is something of which only a very select few are capable... this is not easy at all.

This is an *advanced skill.*

This is what I call *Advanced Magic.*

Giving you the ability to use Magic or the 'law' of attraction consistently, effectively, and *at will* is the purpose of this book.

But as you go through this course, I would like you to move away from the notion of 'the law of attraction'. Yes, I know it's the common and accepted way of speaking about these things. But in many ways, it puts across a misleading impression of what is going on and the way things work.

Because here's the funny thing: as you become more and more adept at creating things, you start to realise that 'making things happen' is not the be-all and end-all. In the beginning, we get hung up on 'attracting things' – more money, a mate, or a particular job. But as you progress and your Magical ability increases, these things become less important and appear almost trivial compared to the greater riches you experience. If this sounds like spiritual self-help flim-flam and flowery words, don't worry... I thought that once.

I promise you: you will come to see that *making things happen* is a bit of a red herring, almost a sham. Wonder, bursting optimism, glowing happiness, and a sense of everything being truly, perfectly okay... all these things are before you. *This is what Magic can bring you.*

Let me be clear: while I consider myself proficient, I'm certainly no expert in this. I still have a long way to go, and a lot of learning lies ahead of me. It is quite possible that with enough attention and dedication, you may become far more powerful than I am and progress even more quickly. You may develop a deeper understanding of Advanced Magic than I have. If you can believe more strongly, be more vigilant, take greater responsibility, and study your experience harder, you may well exceed my still limited ability.

Be warned: this volume may come as a surprisingly dense read in comparison to my other work and may lack some of the 'feel good' aspect of those first books. If you want a quick fix of positive thinking, to be told that using Magic and the Law of Attraction is fast and simple, and anyone can master it with ease, I suggest you *buy a different book*. But if you are serious about mastering Advanced Magic, if you are willing to treat this with the reverence, time, care, and study that it deserves, *do keep reading.*

For those who are ready,

I give you *Advanced Magic.*

4 HOW TO WORK WITH THIS BOOK

I am taking it for granted that you have already read *Becoming Magic* and *Doing Magic*. In writing this book I have assumed knowledge of my previous work and some of the jargon and concepts in this book won't make a lot of sense without it.

Just in case, here is a brief recap…

Becoming Magic was all about preparation – getting you to experience the first inklings of Magic in your life. I advised you to start small, rather than go for your heart's desire up front.

I said that if you go in too high, you will be disappointed or worse. I went through the pitfalls that can befall you if you attempt to do enormous manifestations off the bat – the horror of manifesting the opposite, or worse, the snap-back.

In *Becoming Magic*, I introduced you to the idea that Magic is not something you *do*, but something you *are*. I suggested that if you don't do the preparations and get *you* right first, things could go spectacularly wrong. In order to do this, I said you must make the following preparations:

> 1. Take responsibility
>
> 2. Stop complaining and negativity
>
> 3. Practise gratitude
>
> 4. Notice and take notes

Only when these preparations were complete, did I advise you move on to book 2, *Doing Magic*.

In this part of the course, I told you that there are only two steps to Magic:

> 1. *Ask*
>
> 2. *Receive*

Doing Magic introduced *asking* techniques. But more importantly, it was designed to explain what

I call the *Receiving State*. As soon as you ask, I said you must immediately get out of the way and into *receiving*, because nothing will work until you do. *Receiving* is all about the subtle but essential art of allowing all your desires to flow to you. I explained that it is not the *asking* but the *receiving* that works the magic. I even suggested that a great way of manifesting an exceptional life is not to ask at all, but to move straight into *receiving* and delight in the surprises that come your way. When you have learnt how to correctly and easily access the Magical *Receiving* State, your desires will appear to fall into your lap.

If you have read *Becoming Magic* and *Doing Magic* but have already moved on to this book without having followed any of the instructions in those first two books, without any preparation, without having seen any results, without even getting an inkling of Magic in your life, *don't be surprised if nothing happens.*

These books were always designed to be a *course* in Magic. That means that certain learnings must take place before other lessons are introduced.

'But why didn't you just write one big book containing all the lessons?'

When you become more proficient with Magic, you will understand that it simply wouldn't have been *appropriate* to include all the theory and detail in one go. If I had given you these more advanced ideas in this book up front, it might have been overwhelming. You may also have been tempted to try Advanced Magic off the bat. And without any preparation, you were likely to get bogged down, have poor results, become despondent and so lose trust and belief. And if you don't have *belief*, you are lost. Rather than starting out on your Magical path by working on your heart's desire, trying to do enormous manifestations and spectacular acts of Magic (which almost never work in the beginning), I am a big fan of making slow, but steady and sure progress. Learning bit by bit, increasing your experience, trust, and belief in small, solid increments. Give people too much too soon, and there is always the danger you will blind people with details, bore them with theory, and leave them unmotivated to make those first vital baby steps.

But now, assuming you have followed the steps in *Becoming Magic* and *Doing Magic,* your preparations are complete. At this point, rather than boring and befuddling you, theory and details will act to deepen your understanding, increase your power, and ramp up your Magical ability.

I urge you not to rush, but to read slowly and carefully, sometimes stopping to ponder on what I have said. If I have done my job properly, the experience of reading will make a subtle change in you.

These books are written, not just to be understood intellectually, but also to have a tangible, experiential effect. They are written to draw you effortlessly into the receiving state *and beyond.*

I am hoping, not merely to entertain you for an hour or two, but to create a shift in understanding, in belief, in aspect. If you feel like a change has taken place after reading this book, my work is done. If you feel nothing, then please accept my apologies for wasting your time and move on.

Let me make one important point very clear: what I put forward in this book is *theory.* It is what I suspect to be true given my experience of working with Magic. It is *my* interpretation of events. You may have a different way; others may have a different theory. *And that's all fine.* As I said in *Doing Magic,* different interpretations and descriptions 'speak to' different people, and apparently 'competing theories' are usually just different ways of describing the same thing.

In this book, I am going to show you how *I* have used certain 'Magical' principles to create pretty much everything I could ever ask for. It is not the *only* way, and it may not be the easiest way.

But it was *my* way. And it has absolutely worked for me, time and time again.

'Why only 100 pages long? Surely a book on Advanced Magic should be hundreds, thousands of pages long?'

All of my books are *deliberately* compact. And here's the reason why:

Advanced Magic is probably 10% theory and 90% practise.

My books are intentionally short, because it encourages the reader to go from merely reading *about* Magic to actually becoming and doing it. My books are signposts, nothing more.

I give you these books in small, compact instalments so that you can *experience* those things of which I speak gradually, slowly, surely. This book will lead you through the steps to becoming an Advanced Magician. But, as you go through, you will begin to see and realise more and more that at some point you must put these books down and get on with things yourself.

Look at your own experience. Think about those times when you were able to manifest something perfectly. Think about those times when it all went wrong. Think about those times when you manifested the exact opposite to what you intended.

What was going on for you? What was going on in you? What were you thinking, what were you feeling, what state of mind, mood, energy were you in?

These are the sorts of questions you need to begin asking yourself. This is how you become proficient in Advanced Magic. It is not by reading more or focussing harder or visualising in more detail. It is by getting a sense *of your own Magic.*

You need to know what trust *feels* like. You need to know what conviction *feels* like. You need to see, notice, and experience what goes on in your own mind and body, when a manifestation occurs for you *and you know absolutely that you were the cause of it.*

As these books go on, there will be less feel-good and more depth and understanding. My first books reignited and rekindled, but I can't keep the fire going indefinitely with motivational talk. At some point, you need to put the books down, feel your own Magic, and tend to your own fire.

Don't just follow. Live it. Make it your own.

5 WHAT'S STOPPING YOU?

There are some things that will always stop your Magic from being consistent and reliable, but they are not what you might expect.

The things that stop your Magic from being effective *don't* include: getting techniques wrong, needing to get clarification regarding the minutiae of specific tiny details, or needing to do more reading. All of these things have very little real effect on our Magic, although they tend to take up a lot of our misplaced attention.

In my experience, there are just three main things that get in the way of your Magic:

1. Lack of *belief* in yourself and your ability to do Magic. This includes wondering where your manifestations are or why they haven't arrived yet.
2. Dropping out of the *receiving* state, (usually by worrying, stressing, or complaining when something 'bad' happens or apparently 'goes wrong').
3. Continued *asking*.

So, by interpolation, we could say that the ability to do Advanced Magic can be increased by attending to the following three areas:

1. Increasing *belief*.
2. Coping better with apparent mishaps (and so deepening the *receiving* state).
3. Stopping *asking* (once means *once*).

These are the lessons of this book.

You may have already noticed that these principles are actually intertwined. In some sense, they are all part of the same overall picture. But for the sake of clarity and organisation, it is easier to consider them individually.

In short, the way to Advanced Magic is to stop *asking* and increase your self-belief while deepening your *receiving* state.

Sound straightforward? Don't be fooled.

6 LESSON ONE:

BELIEFS CREATE YOUR WORLD

In the first two books, I told you to forget all about 'thoughts become things' and not to spend too much time consciously focussed on your wants.

Preaching, 'thoughts become things' is a bit like telling people 'you can have anything you want, just as long as you keep your thoughts *on* what you want and *off* what you don't want.' But asking someone not to think of poverty when they are trying to manifest money – it's nigh on impossible. So 'thoughts become things' is like giving someone the means to create anything they want, and then making it impossible for them to do so.

In my opinion, people who tell you to use 'thoughts become things' are wildly underplaying just how difficult this principle is to use. And every unsuccessful attempt to use it only serves to dent your confidence in your ability to do Magic.

I am going to suggest you work on something much more effective than mere thought. I'm going to suggest you work on *belief*. In *Becoming Magic* I said,

"Rather than mere thoughts, it is your deeply held beliefs that have the greatest effect."

Why *belief*?

Well, once you have forged a belief, it will inform, affect, and determine everything you think anyway. It will also inform everything you say, feel, and do. For example, if you have a strong belief that you are rich, you don't have to bother trying to think rich thoughts, feel rich, or act like a rich person. You will do those things automatically.

Thought without belief is ineffectual at best. At worst, it just draws sharp attention to your underlying state of lack and all those associated negative *beliefs*.

This is why most people get negative results with 'thoughts become things'. When you force yourself to think something just in order to manifest it, *it almost never works*. This is because while your daydreams, your musings, and your contrived 'manifestation thoughts' may be on what you *want*, your stronger convictions are that you *lack* it, you don't have it, you need it desperately, and *you may never get it*.

Thoughts without *belief* are daydreams, idle musings, or longings. But thoughts that are informed by your deeply held *convictions* have an entirely different quality about them; it is *these thoughts that have power*.

For your thoughts to have any power to change the world, you need to *believe* them with conviction.

7 THE IMMENSE POWER
OF BELIEF

Let me ask you a question:

Why do you believe the things you do?

For most people, the answer is that they 'believe what they see', or that their beliefs come from their experience of life.

I ask you to accept, at least on faith for now, that things are actually completely the other way around. Your experience of life comes from what you believe. Look around: our lives, by and large, accurately reflect the beliefs we hold.

Beliefs create your world. You don't believe what you see; you *see what you believe.*

'Yeah, yeah. I know all that, I've heard it all before. Everyone says this. I believe that already, but it still doesn't help me.'

The fact is you probably don't believe it at all. You may *suspect* this is true, you may *hope* it's true. And you may really, really *want* to believe it's true. But that doesn't mean you really do believe it as strongly as you believe in your ability to walk or that the sky is blue. Thinking something sounds reasonable or interesting or having 'heard it before' is not the same as belief.

'Beliefs become things' is not just a New Age cliché. This concept needs to be accepted until it becomes conviction – because this is the essence of Magic…

Remember from *Becoming Magic* I told you that you must work on *you* before going near *Doing Magic*. You must become the person you want to be; you must *become Magic,* and the world will respond.

But the type of person you are is intricately tied up with what you believe. Your beliefs inform what you think, do, and say, your tendencies, your preferences, the friends you keep, the job you do, the sensibilities and opinions you hold. You could almost say that you *are* your beliefs!

And as we know, your world is just a reflection of the person you *are*.

So by changing your beliefs, you literally, not merely in some hypothetical, metaphorical or spiritual sense, but *actually and physically* change your world!

What is it that makes the powerful Magician powerful? What is it that sets that person apart from the rest of us? It is nothing mysterious or spooky. It is not that they are 'psychic' or were a high priestess in a previous life.

It is belief. It is complete and utter conviction, in Magic and in their own ability to carry it out. Advanced Magic comes when you move from merely playing around with the Law of Attraction, away from wondering and daydreaming, away from 'testing this out'… and towards *knowing* that this stuff works.

This is about a jump, a shift in aspect, after which you can never see things quite the same way again.

It's about seeing yourself as creator, rather than passive reactor, *not* just reading those words *beliefs create your world* and liking the sound of them, but really, truly believing them.

And here's the really twisty-turny ironic circular bit – the more you come to believe that your beliefs create your reality, the more it becomes true. That means that the stronger you believe in this principle, the stronger, the more *advanced* your Magic. When this belief becomes entrenched, a real conviction, a belief as strong as the sun rising, or that the sky is blue, *then you will enter the realms of Advanced Magic.*

That is the point at which you will be able to pick what you want to be true, and because you *know* absolutely with complete conviction that your belief will create it, *it will start to manifest almost immediately.*

Thus you find it easy to believe whatever you choose. Beliefs are not created by the world – the world is created by your beliefs. When you know this to be true with conviction, changing beliefs is as easy as changing socks.

This really gets the sceptics wound up. Their counter argument comes from scientific methodology and it goes like this…

If we need to believe in a principle to make it true (if it only works for those who believe in it), they claim, this makes it completely unfalsifiable (meaning it is impossible to disprove).

Therefore, according to the sceptics, this principle must be rejected.

But these notions of proof and falsifiability come from science, and as I have pointed out before, if you try to force Magic into a scientific framework, you will come unstuck. It's only if you hold the scientific, empirical view that beliefs are created *by* the world's effect on you that you will even have this problem. If you accept that beliefs create your experience of the world, this whole tension evaporates, along with such unnecessary notions as 'objective proof'.

As far as I see it, there is no problem with having to believe in something for it to be true. In my world, that's all that being true is. Whether it's Magic, God, science or 'what you see with your own eyes', it takes your belief in something to make it true.

Take the anti-religious arch-scientist, Richard Dawkins: If an angel appeared and sat at Richard's dinner table and told him the baby Jesus had a message for him, Dawkins wouldn't suddenly convert to Christianity. He would not believe his eyes. He would assume he was dreaming, hallucinating, or even that he had gone mad. He might not even *see* the angel at all. His belief in science is simply too strong for him to accept what he had seen with his own eyes as truth. And the religious believer does not allow the existence of the scientist's apparent 'facts' to alter their belief in God. For the devout Christian or Jew, the existence of God *is* fact.

Do you remember a time in your life when it felt like you could have and get anything you wanted? Do you remember how you believed in yourself back then? Do you remember how powerful, confident, and immortal you felt as a child, teenager, or young adult?

Do you remember how much you believed in yourself?

We are simply shaking off the years of negativity that you have allowed the world and other people to pile onto you. We are bringing back the self-belief, the confidence that comes from utter conviction. And when that happens, you will shine once again.

So don't skim over this business of *beliefs create your world*. Study it; examine your own beliefs, your own experiences, and your own life until you can see the absolute truth of it. Get the principle of *beliefs become things* so etched into your mind that it becomes a part of who you are.

'But now I feel even more stuck! My belief is that I'm fat, poor, unlucky, and that I don't really believe in any of this Magic stuff, so how on earth can I ever change my life for the better?'

Don't worry: later in this book I will show you a fabulously effective way of replacing your negative beliefs with positive new ones.

8 LESSON TWO: ADVANCED RECEIVING

Here are some things the Advanced Magician will never say or think:

Oh no, why did THAT happen?

What am I supposed to do now?

I can't believe it's gone wrong again

I feel like giving up

I don't think this is working

What am I doing wrong?

Why isn't it working for me?

The final requirement for Advanced Magic is the state of being okay, *completely and absolutely* okay, with anything and everything that may happen. This is intimately tied up with the subject of belief as discussed in the last section; when you deem an event as 'bad' or 'not working' or 'going wrong' or 'a disaster,' it means you are wanting it to be different; it means you want to change it.

But this all means that in some sense you *don't believe* – you don't believe in your own power and ability to achieve things. You don't believe in the Magical process. You don't *trust* that things are going to work out without more intervention.

Let's think about it: when you strongly believe something, you no longer try to make it happen. You just accept; you deeply *trust* that everything will turn out in the expected way. From this point of view, anything that happens appears to be either a stepping-stone or a manifestation itself.

However, if you take issue with any particular event, deem it 'wrong', or as a mistake, or as an example of things 'not working', then you are *not* seeing it as a stepping-stone. You are not believing in your own power, not trusting that everything is working out. You are *wanting* things to be different; you are very much *not okay* with the way things are turning out...

...and when you are *not* okay with the way things are turning out, you snap right out of the Magical receiving state.

The Advanced Magician *knows* that every little thing is working out just perfectly.

The Advanced Magician is even perfectly accepting of the fact that their deepest desires *may never manifest.*

This may sound horribly counterintuitive, even contradictory. After all, if you are trying to *make* things happen, how are you supposed to be fine with the fact that they might not?

By being okay with everything, *even with the non-manifestation of your deepest desires*, you place yourself in the ultimate state of trust and belief. And irony of ironies, all your deepest desires are then all the more likely to come to you.

One of the more delightful consequences of this is that the Advanced Magician knows there is literally *no such thing as a setback.* There are no disasters.

There are only stepping-stones to something greater.

Look for the roses, let everything be okay, don't be impatient, get completely out of the way, *and watch the Magic happen.*

'But I want to make things happen, not just watch them happen.'

And so you will.

The key here is to realise that a lot of what is keeping things you want from you is your worry, your insistence that things turn out a certain way, and more than any of this... *your fear that things will NOT* turn out just as you wanted.

Let me repeat that, because it's vitally important.

Part of what is keeping things you want from you is your fear that you won't get them.

If you are worried or afraid that something might not happen, that your manifestation will not work, it means that in a big sense, you *don't believe* it can or will occur. You are stuck in *asking* for things to be different.

Soon, you can move to seeing that with every occurrence that happens, there are multiple ways to view the situation. When an apparent disaster hits, I'm not saying you should cheer and do a happy dance; I'm just saying you should take one step back and put your focus on where this event may lead you. *Where is the silver lining here? Where are the roses?* They will be there, if only you look hard enough.

The perfect receiving state is one of utter trust that things are working out, of complete conviction in your Magical ability, of not wanting to change a single thing about that present moment, about not needing to do anything, nothing pulling at your attention and making you feel you should be elsewhere. There is no wanting. There is no *asking*.

With practice you can go deeper and deeper, noticing the subtler ways in which there is often a nagging feeling that something is wrong or needs to be changed. Try to see that these nagging wants are usually totally unnecessary. Practise watching them, feeling them, and letting them go. Soon, these lesser wants too will diminish, and you can spend longer and longer in this delicious state.

There are some similarities between this and meditation, but there are some major differences too. The object of this is not to quiet your mind or your thoughts, but merely to stop that nagging wanting that can occupy your entire life. You don't need to sit still with closed eyes and do nothing; you can do this when driving or walking or doing the dishes.

Besides powering up your manifestations, spending time not wanting is a worthwhile pastime in its own right, just because it makes you feel so damned good!

I find this particularly easy at Christmas when there's no email, no business phone calls, nothing to do except enjoy the peace. And when I keep this state up for several days, wonderful manifestations are almost guaranteed to occur. Christmas is doubly Magical for me, because I spend such a large proportion of my time in this fabulous receiving state. As I put the finishing touches to this book, it is mid December, and Christmas is all around me. Everything is going so well for me, it almost doesn't seem fair. Life is simply delicious at the moment. I have never felt the Magic quite as strongly.

Most of us are not able to keep this up at all times. I cannot always keep this up and sometimes lapse into worry and disappointment. Magical purists will tell you even death and disease can be looked upon with detachment and disinterest. I don't see any reason to go that far. I'm still human, and so are you. I still cried when my friend died last year, and I still fear cancer; it hasn't interfered with my ability to do Magic. I'm not saying every person can be fine with unexpected bereavement, not bat an eyelid when love is lost, or not suffer a few sleepless nights if bankruptcy threatens. But being fine, *absolutely fine,* with long queues, high bills, and inconsiderate drivers is a good start!

You don't have to strive for perfection or extremes. You can be an imperfect human being with Magical tendencies and still lead an exceptional life. As long as you do some of this some of the time, you will see results. Do most of it most of the time, and you will see awesome results. If the general direction is positive, this is sufficient to have a really exceptional life.

So don't ever beat yourself up for not being able to do all of it all of the time. Maybe only a dozen people in human history have been able to do that.

You don't have to be a Buddha, Ghandi, or Jesus Christ. You can just be wonderful *you*, warts and all!

And remember: even Jesus lost his temper when greedy moneylenders took over the temple!

9 HOW TO HEAD OFF DANGER

In *Becoming Magic,* I briefly mentioned the extraordinary phenomenon of being able to head off danger by expecting the worst. I suggested that by expecting the worst, far from inviting it into your life, you can actually prevent it happening.

But how on earth does this work?

It is quite straightforward really: by expecting *the very worst* in a calm and considered way, you are, in effect, saying that you are absolutely fine with anything that may happen. If even the very worst is okay with you, then you have no fear. You are okay with the worst, the best, and everything else in between. There are no mishaps; there is no adversity. Everything is okay, even if the very worst occurs. You are in the realm of Advanced Magic, and so 'the very worst' has almost no chance of happening.

> "God sendeth his rain on the just and unjust alike, for evil befalls the righteous and the unrighteous, but it cannot visit him who sees and is convinced of nothing but good."
>
> -Andersen, Uell S. (2011-06-06). *Three Magic Words*

Expecting the worst does not mean sitting and wondering and fretting and anticipating the very worst. This won't do at all! Expecting the worst means looking the worst-case scenario full in the face, thinking of the consequences, and finding a way to be okay with them. Do this well enough, and those worst case scenarios will never find their way into your life.

10 MY PERFECT MANIFESTATION

A particular local charitable cause that is very dear to my heart got into terrible difficulty which threatened to shut them down. They had been the victim of a hateful fraud and couldn't afford legal representation. The police wanted nothing to do with it, dismissing their plight as 'a civil matter'. We were on our own. For a couple of days, I anguished about how to help them. I had given them money hundreds of times, but this was only ever a short-term stopgap. They knew this too. They knew they couldn't continue with me constantly propping them up, and they were considering shutting down their enterprise for good.

I was at a loss how to help them long term, and it was a very stressful time for all of us. I was almost in despair. I was also furious at the injustice of what had happened – how could someone defraud a charity? It was a crime up there with beating a child or stealing from an old lady, and I was eaten up with resentment. It was one of the worst times of my life.

I had temporarily dipped out of Advanced Magic and fallen back into the realms of normal worry, lack of control, fear, and disempowerment.

(This does happen from time to time. It shouldn't worry you, as long as you can get back on track).

It didn't take long for me to get a hold of myself and stop the rot. I stopped, took a breath, and decided it was time to take my own medicine. I used a new version of the 'Letter to the Universe" technique that I detail in *Doing Magic* and asked the Universe to help me manifest a constant source of money for the charity. I poured out onto paper all my feelings of fear, anger, and resentment. I told the Universe about the injustice, the pain created by what had been done. I remember writing about how I would see their delighted faces when I told them everything was going to be fine, how close we would all feel. I printed the letter out, and I instantly shredded it. This was my 'sending'.

I let go and trusted fully that this difficulty was not a setback; it was in fact an absolute triumph. I wasn't sure why yet, but I *knew* deep down it would lead to something wonderful. And because I knew that *if* I believed this, it would be true. The fear left me and I began to look forward to the appearance of the silver lining.

It was in a crisis meeting with the charity that a comment was made to me 'Genny, you are always so positive about things. I love the way you can always look on the bright side and see the good in things. Do you think one day you can teach us how you do that?'

Until that point, I had been afraid to tell anyone about my Magical ability for fear of ridicule. I had experienced the patronising, concerned, pitying, or downright disdainful looks from people before whenever I mentioned 'Law of Attraction'. But this terrible disaster that had befallen my charity was the push that inspired me to take that step. I loved that charity more than I hated ridicule.

It was from that very crisis meeting that the idea came to me to write those first two books, *Becoming Magic* and *Doing Magic*. If you have read them, you will already know that I don't take any personal profit from sales of those books, that they were written to raise money for this local cause.

Those two books were an instant, and I mean *instant*, success. It was quite extraordinary. I had been a writer for almost ten years, but the level of success of *Becoming Magic* left me speechless.

It was often selling hundreds of copies a day, allowing the charity not only to pay the lawyers to sort out the fraud issue, but also to expand and plan for the years ahead. And now, my charitable cause has a constant and permanent flow of money. They no longer need to come to me for hand-outs. They now have the freedom to expand and continue their wonderful work. And that gives me more personal pleasure and purpose than almost anything else I have ever done in my life.

And it all came from the ashes of despair, from a seemingly insurmountable problem. That insurmountable problem turned out to be a stepping-stone to the best thing that had ever happened to them (and one of the best things that has ever happened to me).

When I realised just what a huge success my first two Magic books were turning out to be, I held a meeting with a couple of the charity members. I told them the news of what I had set up and how all their money problems were over. I saw their amazed faces. One of them cried. I felt full of love and utterly complete. We had never been closer as friends.

Months later, while writing *Advanced Magic*, I came across a file on my computer simply called 'Letter'. Upon opening it, I discovered my actual letter to the Universe, written all that time before.

And at that moment, I realised that it had all happened, *exactly* as I had asked for it, down to the meeting where I saw their delighted faces. Even the venue, a big country house with a fire burning, was in my letter.

And the weird thing was, I hadn't even remembered writing these things. I had actually forgotten about this particular manifestation attempt. I knew quickly that by looking for the seed of hope in the ashes of despair, I would find it. But

I had forgotten that I actually asked for it formally in this letter.

It was one of the most flawless manifestations I had ever carried out, being almost word perfect what I had asked for, *and then some!*

But why had this particular manifestation worked out so perfectly, even though I had forgotten all about it?

It is *because* I had forgotten all about it!

If you have any experience of manifesting, you will already be familiar with this phenomenon – the way that things often come to you just when you have stopped wanting them or thinking about them.

So in this case, all the perfect elements were there. I had asked *once* and then immediately 'released' the asking into the aether. I had spent the weeks ever since in a general state of abject *trust*, because that is what I always do when in a crisis situation. Because it was done for others, I had none of the usual grasping need for a certain outcome. If I could raise a few hundred quid, that would be great. If not, nothing much would change. So I had asked, I had got into the receiving state, and I had stayed there.

Must we always forget about our asking in order to manifest? That would be difficult indeed. But it does show the mechanics of the process very clearly. Because I had forgotten the letter, I hadn't once asked when it would be coming or wondered why it hadn't appeared yet. I had not once gone back to 'peek'. I completely and quite perfectly stayed out of the way of the precise details of the manifestation, *because I had forgotten I even asked for them*. And so without interference from me, my wanting, my grasping, and my lack of belief, the Magic was able to work perfectly.

11 LESSON THREE: WHY ASKING IS SUCH A PROBLEM

In *Becoming Magic*, I introduced you to the idea that *wanting* could be viewed almost as the opposite of *having*. In utilising the principle of *thoughts become things* and thinking constantly about your wants, you end up focussed on your state of *lack*, stay stuck in *asking*, and hence prohibit the *having* of your desires. But the situation is actually more complicated than that: it is when there is an underlying *belief* in lack that 'thoughts become things' can be tricky. When you visualise and think continually about your wants, it is this negative underlying belief in lack that is drawn sharply into focus… and *strengthened*.

In light of this, in *Doing Magic* I suggested that one of the best ways to manifest wonderful things is not to focus on wants at all, skip the *asking* stage altogether, and instead move immediately into *receiving*. Rather than asking for specifics, it can be more effective and rewarding just to bask in receiving and wait to see what the world brings you.

But what happens when you successfully use one of the asking techniques in *Doing Magic*? And how does all this fit in with some of the other apparent truths about doing Magic?

For example, how does *letting go of desire* relate to *create your world?* Why is letting go *so* important? What's the mechanism by which it can work? When I carried out my perfect manifestation, how was my letting go and forgetting an instance of *beliefs create your world?* At first sight, letting go doesn't seem to add in any way to a positive belief. It doesn't seem to make you into the person who holds the new belief, and it doesn't make you into someone who thinks, talks, and acts in accordance with that new belief.

In addition to this, my perfect manifestation certainly involved my using 'Asking the Universe'. But how did this work so well if asking itself is such a problem?

It is not asking that's the problem…

It is *continually* asking that's the problem…

Why?

Asking *continually* signifies *lack,* lack of belief that you'll get your desire, and yearning, grasping powerlessness. *Grasping wanting is a negative belief that you may never get your desire.* Letting go thus works to eradicate that *negative belief* associated with wanting.

Asking once with the intention of immediately letting go (as in a Letter to the Universe) is akin to a decision, a direction, a command, taking control, power.

When you ask once, with the full intention of immediately letting go, this has inherent in it a huge amount of belief, trust, and *total conviction that your desire will come to you.*

If you *continue to ask,* you highlight how little you believe in your own Magic and the whole process. A true Advanced Magician does not feebly and imploringly *ask.* A true creator *commands.*

Now we can see that *asking* is a tiny, almost inconsequential, part of the Magical process. All it does is push the focus in a certain direction. *Asking* is done merely in the fleeting moment that you decide you want something. From then on, *receiving* is all there is.

I use the standard phrases like *Asking, Receiving* and *Universe,* because they are handy and familiar ways to refer to what is going on. They make the exposition easier, rather than having to come up with my own terminology. But what is really going on is not anything like 'asking' and 'receiving' in the usual sense of the words. It is not that you are asking some external power to give you something, which that someone then bestows upon you as a gift.

Because, after all, *asking* implies that you aren't the one in control here. It suggests the power is outside of you. When really, it comes from within you.

What is really going on in the process of *Becoming Magic,* in the process of *asking* and *letting go,* is that you are becoming more convinced of your own power and ability. You are starting to believe you will actually receive what you have asked for and are becoming more and more like the type of person who already has those things. And the world, the Universe, life, and other people begin to dance in sync, reflecting and bringing you things befitting the new you and the positive beliefs you now hold.

When you are strongly convinced you will get your desire, there is no need for asking. You still *want* your desire at some level, but you have no fear that you won't get it.

For example, think about the want for a delicious meal you are going to have this evening. Think about how it feels to have your hunger satisfied by this delicious dinner. You are really looking forward to it. You really, really want it. You want it *now,* but you can't have it now. The wanting is thus really strong. But it is a want that comes with absolute *belief* that your want will indeed be satisfied. *There is no asking here.* That part is done.

You have absolute faith, no doubt, conviction. You trust fully that tonight, you will receive the object of your desires. And so you do.

Now compare this feeling to the wanting you feel when you walk past an Aston Martin, or see a couple in love holding hands, or see a perfect body, or see a group of friends having a barbecue on the beach, laughing and having fun while you are poor, overweight, and alone on a Saturday night. It feels longing, grasping, sinking, sad.

Notice the difference? In the second example, you have very little *belief* that that desire will ever come to you. *This* is why it feels longing and grasping, not just excited and expectant. And this is why mere wanting or continually asking will never manifest a thing.

Without belief that you'll get it, the wanting for an Aston Martin just highlights and strengthens your belief that you don't have a nice car, that your current car is old and broken down, that you're not the kind of person who could even dream of owning the Aston. You are stuck in asking. And whereas asking *with belief* is akin to a command done only once, asking with *no* belief is akin to a pleading, an imploring, a disempowered, disbelieving act of begging. It is usually done continually.

So, it's not wanting, *per se*, that is the opposite of having. Rather than *any* wanting, it is actively yearning, pushing, striving, and *asking for things to be different* that is the opposite of having. It is *this* wanting (with its inherent negative beliefs) that we must let go.

Strong belief and *non-grasping want* are two sides of the same coin

Lack of belief and *grasping want* are two sides of another coin

Thus *letting go* of grasping wants is equivalent to *increasing belief*.

TO RECAP AND BRING IT ALL TOGETHER...

I suggested that there were three things that may stop your Magic from being successful:

> 1. Continually asking

> 2. Not believing in yourself

> 3. Not 'being okay' with everything that happens

So, summing everything up...

Asking ONCE, strong belief, feeling powerfully Magic, letting everything be okay, and *non- grasping wanting* go hand in hand with successful manifestation.

Asking CONTINUALLY, lack of belief, feeling powerless, not *letting everything be okay,* and *grasping wanting* go hand in hand with unsuccessful manifestation or even manifestation of unwanted things.

The most impressive and spectacular manifestations happen when you ask *once* with huge belief and then immediately let go and settle into the receiving state. This means being okay with every little thing that then befalls you, *even with the non-manifestation of your dearest desire.*

And once again we have that torturous dichotomy between commanding on the one hand and letting everything be okay on the other. Really successful Advanced Magic is about plotting a way through the tangled incongruity of both desiring and directing a certain outcome and being totally, *completely* okay with it never happening. I cannot show you exactly how to do it. But find a way you must.

This is wisdom. Set your course, steer it right and you will become more powerful than you ever thought possible.

12 HOW TO CHANGE BELIEFS

For some, this business of 'letting go of wants' remains nigh on impossible. If your belief is currently very low, you may feel like you are simply kidding yourself when you attempt to let go. Perhaps you would *like* to believe in Magic and your own power, but the larger part of you is sceptical. Are there some desires that just won't leave you alone, nagging constantly at your awareness? Do you just feel utterly stuck in *asking*?

As we know, when you ask, you *must* then let go of asking and move swiftly into receiving. Best of all is to forget you even asked in the first place.

My most impressive manifestations have usually been done this way.

But…

… this can be prohibitively difficult, especially if the thing you want feels like a desperate *need*. After all, it's not easy to decide consciously to 'forget' about something you *don't* want, let alone something you want very much.

There is another way…

Rather than futile attempts deliberately to 'forget' your desires, I'm going to suggest you do the opposite and actually embrace them. But I want you to think about these wants in a very different way, without longing or lack. This will act subtly to increase your belief, both in your own magical ability, and in the likelihood that the desires will come to you. At the same time, you will weaken your current belief in your state of lack. If you can think about your desires in the right way, something wonderful will happen: rather than highlighting and reinforcing underlying negative beliefs, you will begin replacing them with more positive ones.

So how do we do this? Well, rather than just making a decision to believe in Magic, for example (which is nearly impossible), it is far more effective to *slowly* and *gradually* increase your belief.

Please understand: when you first attempt to actively believe something new, it will almost always feel contrived and forced. It may even feel like you are lying to yourself. But sooner or later, things begin slowly to change...

1. Doubt about your old conflicting belief starts to creep in
2. You start to have an inkling that the new belief may be true
3. You see instances of the new belief being true.
4. The instances increase
5. You know the new belief to be true
6. It becomes a conviction

The simplest, surest, and absolute best way of increasing belief, both in your magical ability and in the likelihood that your desires will come to you, is to start noticing evidence of your manifestations appearing in your life. This helps to counter your scepticism with little bits of positive evidence to the contrary. This may not create massive, spectacularly fast manifestations, but it does work slowly, surely, and fantastically well.

You can use this to work on belief in yourself, your magical ability, and in the whole process of Magic.

Or...

You can use it when working on specific manifestations, to counter feelings of lack and so increase belief that your particular desire is on its way.

Best of all is to do *both!*

Of course, when trying to cultivate a belief, you almost *always* experience evidence that opposes it. Your job is to ignore or explain away all evidence that contradicts your belief, and exaggerate and focus on all the evidence that it is true. When things don't seem to be turning out right, find a way, *any* way, to see them either as positive evidence or as stepping-stones to something greater.

But that's irrational!

In my opinion, rational thought is hugely over-rated! How much Magic, inspiration, creativity, and stuff of immeasurable value has been wasted and lost in the name of rationality?

The truth is, rationality doesn't even come into it. It is not evidence that contradicts the existence of Magic; it is your reaction to that apparent 'evidence' that makes Magic real or not for you.

Let me give you an example...

One of my very good friends, Ella, is an extremely spiritual person. A few years ago she began to worry me. She seemed to be having delusions of grandeur, believing that she was meant for bigger and better things. She saw herself as a true guru, and her desire was to become a great spiritual teacher. All this was fine. But on my last meeting with her, she had come to see every tiny thing as evidence, as a 'sign'. A butterfly landing on her was a sign. A bus going past with a particular word on it was a sign. The waitress bringing the wrong food was a sign that things were turning out just as she expected. Everything that happened was evidence of her great plan unfolding. Greatness was coming to her. It was her right, her destiny.

But what was really worrying was that she was overlooking all those other bits of evidence that clearly contradicted her belief. *I* could see that she was just picking and choosing random events and interpreting them as evidence. *She was being irrational.* Why couldn't she see this?

For the first time I began to become truly worried that Ella had gone mad. There was evidence of mental illness in her family, and I did wonder if I was witnessing her breakdown.

Fast forward a few years, and Ella has become everything she wanted to be. She now runs her own retreats and has thousands of devotees. She is changing lives everywhere for the better. Her grand plan came to be, just as she believed it would. I no longer feel I have the right to judge her as mad, as delusional, or even as misguided or naïve. She has manifested her wildest dream.

I went from secretly and condescendingly judging Ella to wondering how I could learn from her to achieve my *own* deepest wishes. So I began to do what Ella did. I began to look for evidence of what *I* wanted to manifest.

That's when I came up with the idea of the evidence journal.

13 KEEP AN EVIDENCE JOURNAL

You probably know by now that I am a big fan of notebooks and journals. I like to choose beautiful hard-backed notebooks and keep them in my handbag at all times. You probably have already had some success using the gratitude journal I described in the first book.

I now want you also (or instead) to keep an *evidence* journal. A small notebook that fits in your handbag, pocket, or briefcase is ideal for this.

Every day, on a new page, write down the state of affairs you wish to be true. For example:

I am becoming more Magical every day

I am truly Magically powerful

I weigh nine stone

I have a wonderful set of new friends

My illness is leaving me

I'm getting healthier every day

I'm getting richer every day

Don't get too hung up about the phrasing of the statements. It doesn't much matter whether you say, 'I have', or 'it's coming to me', or something else. Some other writers recommend saying, 'I allow myself to have/do/be....'

Personally, this way of putting things does nothing for me. 'I allow myself' sounds like a wimpy, flabby, passive sort of statement. Plus, it's harder to find evidence for the fact that you are 'allowing' something to happen. What would this evidence even look like?

Other gurus advise long and detailed statements such as

'*I easily and gratefully allow my business to becoming thriving and successful for the good of all*'..

I would never have any success with such a long-winded and clumsy statement. It's just not an easy belief to get your head around. I would rather cut straight to the point with *my business is thriving* or even *my business receives thirty orders a day.* Those seem to me beliefs really worth having.

But what matters more than any of this is not what I think, but what *you* think. Use just the phrasing that sounds right and motivational to *you.* It needs to get to the heart of your desire. If you like the sound of 'I allow myself...,' or if you prefer long detailed statements, then that wording *is absolutely right for you.*

I am actually tweaking a technique I referred to as 'Earl Nightingale's Secret' in *Doing Magic,* in which I told you to write down your desire every day. Many similar methods involve your simply writing the statement down over and over, sometimes also repeating it out loud or to yourself, whenever you remember. You may also remember that I said very few people can make this work successfully.

Napoleon Hill suggests powering up the process by feeling 'burning desire' every time you read your statement of intent. Perhaps I have misunderstood Napoleon Hill, but I have *never* had any success with burning desire! To my mind, burning desire equates to constant asking and overwhelming, overpowering *lack*.

To make this work really well, we need to get the constant asking *out* of the process.

Perhaps, like me, you have found these sorts of techniques to be a *torturously slow and difficult* way to do things, particularly if all they do is reawaken your wanting and desperate need.

And if your current strong belief is the complete opposite to your desired state of affairs, that little voice will just keep jumping in with *'There's nothing coming to you – you're flat broke. You're fat and ugly. You have no friends. You are sick as a dog.'*

So we add another step…

…we immediately shut that voice up and counter those negative beliefs by *looking for evidence to the contrary*.

Underneath your statement, you will write down evidence, *any* evidence, that the goal is coming or has already come to you. I usually write 3-6 statements each time.

In the beginning, this may not be easy; some of the evidence might be extremely flimsy. For example:

'I found a pound in my pocket this morning; this must be a sign that I am becoming richer.'

'My skin looked good this morning; that means my soul mate is on his/her way.'

You can work on increasing belief in particular wants, such as the fact that money is coming to you, you are making friends, or you are becoming irresistible to the opposite sex. But even more powerful is to also work on increasing belief in your own Magical ability. See *every* fortuitous event as evidence of your increasing Magical ability. *And that power will increase dramatically.*

For example:

'I feel really good today, I am definitely becoming more Magical.'

'I manifested a parking space perfectly this morning. I'm becoming stronger with my Magic.'

The evidence statements will sound silly and contrived in the beginning, but that's fine. I promise you: keep this up and before long the evidence will become less flimsy, easier to find, and more abundant. The evidence statements will then become less tenuous and more genuine. For example:

'My clothes felt so much looser today. I am definitely losing weight.'

'I have come up with a clear plan for increasing sales. My success is inevitable.'

'My boss gave me a commendation this morning. I'm going to go far in this company.'

'John blushed when he spoke to me today. I am so much more attractive these days.'

'I have seen my first genuine manifestation.'

These statements *must* come from you. Don't copy mine or look for guidance from someone else. This simply won't work. These statements must be genuine examples of *your* looking around for evidence *in your own life* and finding it. *My* answers will not increase your belief. *Yours will.*

This process works to add the vital element of slowly increasing belief.

It quietens all those negative counterexamples that your mind will try to come up with.

It makes you *feel good*, motivated, powerful, like something is happening.

It works to slowly but genuinely and solidly increase your belief in the truth of that state of affairs.

The evidence journal can also be used to explain away any apparent misfortune or 'negative' evidence. It will help you to look at that misfortune, and, rather than panic and fall into despair, *see the roses.* Thus, while the evidence journal draws attention to your want or goal, it encourages you to think about it only in positive ways, never feeling *lack.* It can also be used to note evidence of your increasing power, any serendipitous occurrences, or fantastic insights.

There is only one rule. Never write negatives:, no moaning, no criticisms, no worries, no flimsy hopes. This is not a diary. It is a tool for increasing belief.

The point of this process is *not* to remind yourself of your desire or to tell the Universe how much you want something. It is taking you beyond wanting, into believing. It is taking you from yearning after something to believing it's genuinely and obviously on its way, or even that it's partly already here. And soon, you will no longer have to contrive to believe; evidence that your desire is coming to you will be incontrovertible.

And when that happens, the desired state of affairs begins to enter your life, almost imperceptibly, *effortlessly*.

It seems too simple to be effective, too silly, almost childish. But it *works!* I have used this over and over, with great results. Earl Nightingale suggests doing this for 30 full days. I have usually found it now only takes around 20 days to work, when done properly and consistently. Be vigilant with this technique, and just watch in wonder as things unfold.

14 TALKING YOURSELF INTO MAGIC

You can also add to your belief as you go through the day. Decide what you want to believe. *Eg, I am receiving £10,000. My soul mate is on his way to me. My Magic is increasing all the time. My dream house is coming to me. I am a rich and successful artist/author/architect/teacher/plumber.*

Start telling that story, to yourself and others. Look for evidence that it's true and ignore or explain away all evidence to the contrary. Interpret everything in terms of the new story. Keep your evidence journal every day.

By being like Ella, seeing every butterfly, every waft of wind, every little thing as a sign that things are going your way, you get into step with the world. Not efforting *against* it, but dancing with it!

This is how you dance with life. This is how you get in step with the world.

This is actually the complete opposite of the way most people live their lives. When tiny bits of good fortune appear in a person's life (the beginnings of a manifestation), rather than concentrate on them or see them as evidence of things going well, most people tend rather to *explain them away!*

When a man asks you out, do you think '*It probably won't work out. I don't think he's the marrying kind. He'll probably dump me after a couple of weeks. I'm sure he's only after one thing. Maybe he's doing it for a dare. I expect he just feels sorry for me.*'?

When some money comes into your life, do you think, '*That was lucky. I had better make sure I don't lose it. I had better spend it carefully as I probably won't get another break like this again soon.*'?

When you lose weight, do you think, *'God knows how that happened. I have been a pig lately. I think those scales must be dodgy.'*?

Do you see how we talk ourselves out of Magic?

Rather than explaining success *away*, explain it as obvious evidence of your growing power, your Magical ability, and the fact that everything is turning out for the best.

Does this sound stupid, ridiculous, unscientific, or even crazy? There is no reason why it should; after all, this is what every single person does with every single one of their firmly held beliefs every day.

Human beings don't *see'* an objective and complete picture of 'reality'. They couldn't possibly. It is absolutely impossible for you to process every bit of information that reaches your eyes, ears, and thoughts. Everything that enters your senses is interpreted by your beliefs, whether you like it or not.

We all tend to notice, focus on, and exaggerate those things that confirm our firmly held beliefs. And we tend to gloss over, ignore, deny, explain away, *or not even notice* all those many, many things that contradict our beliefs. This is how our experience of life becomes shaped. This is how we pick our way through the myriad of sense experiences every day.

We *have to pick and choose.* All I am saying is that you begin to pick and choose what you pick and choose!

I have included this idea as part of *Advanced Magic,* because while it seems simple, it takes real vigilance to keep up. You have to have immense faith and the strength of will to push on through all sorts of evidence to the contrary. Don't be the person who constantly stops to ask why it's not working, because you must trust that it *is always working,* no matter what befalls you along the way.

This is what I do, every time. It works, every time.

Once your positive belief becomes strong enough (and this is usually short of a conviction, just a hunch is often enough to see results), that thing *will* appear in your life!

When it does, you won't be surprised that it does. You won't be shocked or astounded. You might not even notice it. Because your belief is already so strong, it comes as no surprise when your life starts moving more and more in the direction of your desires.

The more habitually you do this, the easier it becomes. These days, I just decide that something should happen and start looking around for evidence that it's true, no matter how tenuous or flimsy. Almost always, I can see evidence immediately. And because I have had success in the past, and because I know how well this works, *I find it easier to believe off the bat.* This is a large part of why manifestations now happen for me very quickly. The more successful you are, the easier you will be able to believe at will, and so the more successful you will become!

Just make the decision to start believing the new belief, and start to live your life according to the new story. You have already inadvertently chosen your story through life. It's time to choose a better story. Begin to think, act, and speak like the person who has what you want. Live your life from this new place *always.*

15 THE ISSUE OF VIGILANCE

Why is it that you can read a book like *Becoming Magic*, get all fired up, start a gratitude journal, stop complaining, and begin to see little things changing, little bits of good fortune coming to you...

And then

...it all seems to grind to a halt?

Things start returning to normal. The magic stops. Something bad happens. You feel it's all broken or gone wrong.

Why does this happen?

It's because you have let things go. You may have fallen back into complaining or stopped feeling grateful. You are no longer looking for the good in all things, and you are almost certainly not 'letting everything be okay'. You have fallen back into wanting and worrying.

People often write to me saying:

'I was doing really well, feeling so positive. I had stopped complaining, and everything felt different. But then X happened, and it all went to pot. I started complaining again, and now I feel like I've ruined everything.'

Please understand: this happens to *everyone*. I can't believe the way that people just turn around and give up at this point. (Well actually I can, because this was exactly the way I used to be.)

So what should you do when things go wrong and keep on going wrong? You carry on, of course!

You learn from the experience, grow stronger, set a fresh course, and set sail! If you feel it's all not working, and you want to ask me all sorts of questions about why it's not working, or why it's stopped working, then this is clear evidence that you are not letting things be okay.

You have to be vigilant.

You have to be consistent.

You have to keep it up.

You have to notice, learn, record, adjust.

You have to work at this, *always, constantly.*

'But it's hard!'

Yes, I know it's hard! But be reasonable! We are talking about becoming an advanced wizard! It has taken me years of near-obsession with Magic to come up with what I have. And even I am far from being an expert in this. We aren't talking about picking up some silly little skill or learning a fun hobby. We are talking about becoming proficient in Advanced Magic! Wouldn't you expect something like this to be difficult, to take a long time, to take dedication, commitment, and vigilance? Yes, it's hard. But my goodness, it's worth it!

Because we are so used to being able to pay a price and get something easily, our tendency is to demand things instantly. We want to be able to manifest *now*. We want that thing within days, preferably before we have even finished reading the book. Techniques? Instructions? Those can come later. We will come back to that bit. So we read our book, get all hyped up, follow none of the instructions, and then complain when it doesn't work.

That is not how Magic works.

While I now consider myself fairly proficient in Advanced Magic, it has been a long learning. For as long as a couple of years, I continued to get strangely inconsistent results.

The reason I continued from this place was my absolute *belief* that Magic was possible. Having seen it work once, twice, I would not stop until I found a way to become more skilled with using it. I knew that 'being okay with the way things turn out:' was an essential part of Magic. So I worked diligently not to let things bother me, even when apparent disasters befell me. Mark my words: this was *not* easy in the beginning (it isn't always easy now), but I stuck with it because I knew I must. In the first year, there were many times when I lapsed back into complaining, into worrying about how things were turning out, into trying to force things to happen... and so my results were inconsistent.

But as the non-complaining, and the not worrying, and the being okay all became *habitual*, my Magic became gradually more consistent. Magic was no longer something I was playing with. Magic was becoming my entire life. I didn't just stop complaining when I wanted to manifest something. I stopped complaining all the time. I didn't just look for the roses when manifestations didn't work out. I made sure I was okay with *everything* that happened, whether or not I was working on a particular manifestation at the time.

Many people do really, really well following the Magical principles with regard to a particular manifestation. For example, when trying to manifest money, they are absolutely fine when an unexpected bill comes in. They see it as a stepping-stone, nothing more. However, they still sulk when a work colleague 'borrows' their milk from the staffroom fridge, are incensed that the TV programming schedule has changed, or furious when stuck in a traffic jam.

Don't just follow the principles of Magic when you are trying to make something happen. If you really, seriously are committed to making this work, then you need to make Magic your life.

Remember from *Becoming Magic* that we do not perform Magic on the world; it is not a separate thing to be picked up and used when needed. Magic is something you *are.* This means you need to work on being Magic *all the time,* not just when you need more money or a new car.

GIVE IT A REST

I strongly suggest that for one week of every month you stop all your manifestation attempts, thoughts, and activities. Just stop. Stop keeping the journal. Stop reading. Just totally let go. Don't even worry about keeping your thoughts positive; just go back to your usual self. Give up on all this Magical stuff and go back to normal life.

Ironically, during or shortly after this week is often when wonderful manifestations will occur. But don't spend this week waiting for the manifestations to occur – this will only keep them at bay. Just put Magic out of your head completely.

Sometimes when we are trying hard to stay positive, be grateful, look for evidence, and stay in the right *receiving* state, we actually just become obsessed and begin focussing too hard, trying too hard. This can all work to prevent our Magic from working. We get to the point where we aren't even aware how hard we are working, and don't even notice how hard we have been trying until we stop. This week off is really useful as a sort of 'reboot', allowing us to get back to baseline and then start afresh.

16 LIVING AN EXCEPTIONAL LIFE

Advanced Magic is not about clicking your fingers and making elephants appear or disappear. It is not even about doing bigger and better and faster manifestations. While all these things tend to happen when you become more advanced with Magic, these are not the defining characteristics.

Manifestations are great, but thinking Advanced Magic is all about bigger and faster manifestations of cars and money is missing out the more extraordinary part.

Just imagine for a moment that you could know that *everything* was going to be okay, *really okay*. Imagine you could know that everything was turning out exactly right, for the best. What is 'more stuff' compared to the feeling that everything, *everything* is right?

The signature state of Advanced Magic is the state of absolutely no doubt and no *fear*. It is when you feel so okay with the way your life and events are turning out, that nothing, *nothing* can faze you.

How good would it feel to know that nothing would ever go wrong again, *ever*?

This really can be your reality.

See apparent disasters as stepping-stones and nothing can ever go wrong again.

*'But, you're not talking about things **actually** turning out better; it's just you choosing to see them that way.'*

What constitutes 'turning out better' other than the way you see things? And what would be the point in things being an 'actual' way if you didn't see them that way too?

In the film *Shallow Hal*, Jack Black's character, Hal is given a gift by Anthony Robbins: he begins to see good and kind people as beautiful and bad, selfish people as ugly. He begins a relationship with a beautiful girl and falls in love, not knowing that in reality she is hugely overweight. No matter – in his eyes she is stunningly beautiful. The main moral message of the film is a little confused and questionable, but the point I want you to see is the following: what difference does it make to Hal if the world sees Rosemary as unattractive *if he sees her as beautiful?*

When Ella believed she was divinely inspired, who was I to tell her she was delusional?

If *you* feel that things are going well, whose business is it to tell you otherwise?

If *you* think things are turning out perfectly, then they *are* turning out perfectly. And I mean this literally.

Advanced Magic is not about forcing yourself to carry on through adversity. It's about realising *there is no such thing as adversity.*

When this finally, genuinely hits you, you have no more worry, you have no more fear, and you are free. And your life becomes one big game where nothing can shake you from your position of happiness and power.

TO LIVE AN EXTRAORDINARY LIFE

1. Don't complain, criticise or moan.
2. Practise gratitude.
3. If you ask, move into *receiving* as soon as possible.
4. Look for evidence of your manifestations and of your increased Magical ability.
5. Use an evidence journal to slowly increase belief.
6. Tell a new story in keeping with your new positive belief.
7. Always, always, *always* let everything be okay.

Soon, *the glimpses will come.*

You will begin to notice short periods, seconds or minutes, where you get a sense that you are truly in control, when everything is okay, where nothing could possibly faze you, when you feel that sparkling Magic aliveness – *when you feel Advanced Magic.* You are starting to believe. A sudden glimpse of a new, alternative life flashes into your consciousness, like a memory. The vision of this life is exquisite, like paradise.

And then you will lose it and dip back into normal life with its worries and concerns.

But once you have seen and felt this state, something inside you changes. If you have believed in your own Magic, just for a second, it never really leaves you. This memory will remain, and each time you access the state again, it grows stronger. The memory becomes a constant companion in your life.

The glimpses become more frequent, until this lovely state becomes commonplace. Things start turning out just your way. Miracles start appearing in your life.

And it begins to snowball. Memory turns to conscious awareness. Conscious awareness turns to unconscious awareness. And then, Magic is your life.

GENEVIEVE DAVIS

To be kept up to date with details of my new releases, updates and news please drop me an email and ask to be added to my readers' list. I never spam and promise to keep your details confidential.

Email:
genevievedavis@outlook.com

Facebook:
https://www.facebook.com/pages/Becoming-Magic/741339189264947

Made in the USA
Middletown, DE
02 July 2020

11671025R00066